Saved by God, Kept by Faith

Encouraging Words for Discouraging Times

EBENEZER TYNER III

DEDICATION

I would like to give all praise and honor to my Lord and Savior Jesus Christ. Thank you, Lord, for allowing me to go through the struggles and storms in my life that have made me stronger. Thank you, Lord, for all the lessons that have turned into blessings. You have kept me and blessed me to be a blessing to others.

I dedicate this book to every person God has added in my life; you all have been a great blessing to me. First, to my amazing wife, Latonia Tyner. Throughout our marriage, she has been my confidant, encourager, strength, influencer, love, and a true blessing. Even through the tough times, when I wanted to give up, she was right there to cheer me on. I love you, Latonia, and I thank God for placing you in my life. To my wonderful parents, Mr. and Mrs. Ebenezer Tyner Jr. and Lorraine Tyner, whom I thank for this life, for loving, nurturing, and teaching me how to be the man and the person God has called me to be, and for teaching me about the Lord at an early age. I thank God for them both and I love them. I want to thank my siblings, family members, and friends for all their love and support throughout my life. They all are a true blessing.

I also dedicate this book to my spiritual leaders, Apostle and Pastor Dr. Jeffery Chapman Sr. and First Lady Sandie Chapman, for teaching me and showing me how to live life God's way, for praying for me and prophesying over my life. Dr. Chapman, thank you for the prayers, inspiration, and personal conversations you continue to have with me. You have shown me how to be a great man of God, how to love and serve God in a mighty way, how to overcome fear, doubt, and uncertainty, and most of all, how to trust in God. Thank you, Pastor Ronnie L. Evans, for your prayers and support during the early struggles and storms in my life, you are a great mentor and leader. Thank you to those of you who have prayed for me, encouraged me, and inspired me throughout my life. Lord, I thank you, for placing these incredible people in my life. They have truly been a blessing to me and my journey through life. Therefore, I am blessed to be a blessing to others.

I know that opportunities do not come often, and when they do, we need to take advantage of the ones that God places before us. I am truly grateful for this chance to share my story in hopes that it may be a blessing to someone who may be enduring a battle in their life—whether emotionally, spiritually, or physically. I encourage you to trust in the Lord, never give up, pray without ceasing, and please seek professional help if needed.

TABLE OF CONTENTS

PREFACE

It goes without saying that life is hard. Most of the time, it is *really hard*. For many people, this is probably an understatement especially during this unprecedented time in American history when we are challenged to keep thousands of people from dying from the deadly contagion COVID-19 against a backdrop of maddening events. Here is the landscape of things as I was finishing up this manuscript—violent riots clashing with peaceful protests over social justice issues, millions of people losing their jobs and going on unemployment in record numbers, a congress stalling rather than pressing forward on measures that significantly impact our daily lives, and a first-time sitting commander-in-chief threatening to remain in office even if he loses an historic upcoming election. And let us not forget the many lives that continue to be questionably taken because of their ethnicity. We need to preserve our peace and inner strength when things spin out of control at rapid speed. Hence, I wrote this book.

For a few years, I have enjoyed a growing following on my Facebook page where I encourage people to endure whatever life brings (more specifically, what God Himself causes or allows). Many people have confessed to me that things are not getting any easier for them—something to which I am no stranger. I know how hard it was for me to persevere during a low, low point in my life which I will share in the next chapter. There were times I thought about how easy it would be just to end things once and for all. That is, until I found peace with God and His word.

Writing this book has been cathartic for me in a sense, though it took more than *two* years to finish the manuscript and finally get it to my editor! There were so many challenges during the process of writing, such as fighting back writers' block, editing, writing some more, and passing my corrections back and forth to my editor for yet more editing. What a seesaw of events that turned out to be, but everything was so worth it. I now have a myriad of encouragements on different themes all in one place, where it can be utilized by not only my social media friends but also you. I especially urge you to pay close attention to the Scriptures that are mentioned and spend quiet time reading and re-reading them. In fact, I encourage you to read and study the chapters from which they are extracted. I base a lot of my encouraging comments on scripture because there is no getting around this fact: *God's word* is what brings the peace and inner strength needed to counter anxiety and other negative emotions that arise from situations that are totally out of our control.

I challenge you to not give up and not give in to storms or situations that come in your life. No one said life would be easy, so we will have those difficult periods; therefore, remember that they are only tests. We need to take those experiences and learn from them. God loves you, and He will never do anything to hurt you. Continue to trust in Him through it all.

Finally, as a recovering alcoholic and a former patient of mental illness, I pray that this book will touch the hearts and minds of those who may be going through a battle that seems winless and endless. I pray that the manifestation of God's healing touches your mind and frees you from bondage. Be encouraged. There is victory in Jesus.

CHAPTER 1

Picture This: My Life before Christ

When I joined the U.S. Army, I thought it would be the last place I would see something like alcohol consumed and made available so freely to people looking for a quick, cheap high and fun times. After all, the army is supposed to be a place where discipline reigns supreme, right? It was a very disciplined place but, I was Nineteen and naïve, I did not see the harm in drinking, since it added to the fun for a lot of soldiers, who were trying to deal with life in the army while being miles and miles away from home. At the time, I did not drink nearly as much as my buddies *and* superiors, not realizing that a weekend of drinking beer would eventually lead to hardcore drinking down the road. In fact, before joining the army, I was not what you would call a heavy drinker. Back home, I would drink a few beers with the guys now and then, but not in routine. So, during those days in the army, alcohol was not exactly my 'go to' as much as it was for others in my outfit. Still, I was naïve and did not see the huge destruction that a "little drinking" would bring to my life.

Like I said, there was no real consequence to drinking—or so I thought. An unfortunate turn of events proved me so wrong. The worst came after my retirement from the army after twenty-one years of service. It was a bittersweet day because I would not only begin a new life outside the army but also leave some of my drinking buddies behind. Anyway, as I returned home to smiling, welcoming faces, something inside of me was beginning to die—my soul and will to live. Since my release from the army where I served so many years became a reality. The little drinking, I did do became more and quite constant. As I write this chapter, I am remembering how it did not take long to graduate from one or two drinks over the weekend to multiple shots before the weekend was out. I began hanging out more and more with people I had hung around before joining the army. Eventually, drinking became the norm during the week. It was not unusual for me to wake up half-drunk, get dressed half-drunk, go through my day half-drunk and then, finish out the day fully drunk. The following day, the cycle repeated. I could not handle simple things like having conversations with family and friends without blowing up at them and then using alcohol to calm my nerves. I dared to fight anybody who disagreed with me, including my then wife and kids. To make matters worse for them, I would skip out on them any time I wanted, which was way too often.

If you were to ask anyone who knew me in those days, they would probably tell you that I was out of my mind. They were right; I could not get a handle on my thoughts or my emotions. Both were out of control.

You would think that nearly losing my family was enough of a wake-up call, but it was not. It would take a nasty low for me to come to myself. My then wife had enough of living with an alcoholic husband and eventually, she filed for divorce, I also lost close family members I was devastated. The divorce became the most difficult event I would ever get through, because we had a daughter together. In time, I began slipping into depression and onto an emotional roller coaster. Holding down even one job was a joke. Drinking failed to relieve me of bad memories and left me with a feeling of instability. The depression became so intense that I contemplated various ways to commit suicide to end the misery that had started with one drink intended to solve so many problems. Every waking day was met with a depression that deepened to the point where I had to swallow my pride and seek help or else it would be too late.

There was something else I had to come to grips with: my situation was not just a mental one. It was spiritual as well. That meant my journey out of alcoholism and depression had to include the High King of Heaven—Jesus Christ. I always knew God existed, but I did not have a relationship with Him. And, if I wanted any earthly treatment to take permanent effect, I knew I had to include God in the programming to a better, healthier life. So, I did what every one of you will have to do at some point in your life if you ever want to move from instability to peace. While lying flat on my back one day, I made this confession: "Jesus," I said, "I can't do this anymore. You're going to have to save me from me because I can't." During those times when we are battling circumstances, dear friends, we must be willing to confess to God our faults and ask Him to take over. He is waiting to hear the words "I can't, but You can." Do not be ashamed to speak them, for He already knows that what you are trying to endure is too much for you but not for Him. You will see in later chapters that a quality of God is that He can carry what you cannot *because He is God*. Once I believed in Jesus as my salvation from everything, I settled into the programs that helped with alcoholism and depression. In time, I was healed from both, and I looked forward to experiencing everyday God gave me. And, in turn for His goodness in my case, I learned to be an encourager to those struggling to overcome their own circumstances.

By no means has my journey been easy. It would be misleading to indicate otherwise; however, with Christ, *how* I perceive circumstances has made a difference to my outlook on life and it will for you, too.

CHAPTER 2

The Attributes of God

At the suggestion of my editor, I included this chapter because unfortunately, there are way too many people who say they follow God and his Son, the one and only Jesus Christ, yet have little idea of what He is really like. Therefore, they lack because they lack an understanding of the One, they serve. His very character eludes them. So, before I extend an encouraging word, I want everyone reading this book to understand that God is not some abstract, mindless personality hanging out in the far reaches of space. As you understand His attributes, you will begin to appreciate that He is God. Further with an understanding (as much as we can understand God, that is) of the person of God and his son Jesus, you will begin to understand why you can have peace when everything else around you can be in utter chaos.

In the preface, I mentioned that you should read his word when you are seeking peace and strength. One reason is because His very personality is wrapped up in His word. God is His word, and His word is He. They are not distinct from one another. With that said, let this sink in: God's word is truth. Therefore, He is Truth. Always. He does not lie (Numbers 23:19) and because He is also holy, He is incapable of lying. This brings me to another of his attributes—his holiness.

Where God is concerned, holiness is not some hundreds-year-old movement first espoused by Pentecostals. It is absolute perfection and a quality that is central to His own personality. In the scheme of things, holiness is how He deals with every-thing and everyone. None of God's created beings have abso-lute perfection. This is imperative to remember because even the saved are not without sin. In fact, inherent sin will continue to be present in our lives until the coming of Christ. Now I write all this to point out something essential: God has set a standard for living a life that He says must be set apart from the world. There are some of us trying to overcome this and have peace, while simultaneously disregarding. If you expect peace "that surpasses all understanding" (Philippians 4:7), then you will not experience it if you disobey the God. It is just not going to hap-pen, friend. And I would be equally irresponsible if I encourage you in your sin, so therefore let me be clear. Because God is holy, He *will not* ignore disobedience. Rather, in His holy anger, He will indeed deal with rebellion. With that said, always check your life against the word of God and your relationship with His Son. While holiness is not inherent for God's created beings, the word of God nevertheless commands us to strive for it (1 Peter 1:16) because He is holy. Therefore, repent of any wrongdoing and return to fellowshipping with Christ. Then the peace you seek will be given to you.

God is good. In His word, Jesus tells us that only God is good (Luke 18:19) and in John's letter, we read that there is no darkness in Him (1 John 1:5). So, what does this mean, and what does His goodness have to do with how we can proceed in life? To say that God is good means that He will always act in accordance with what is right and good—again using His own standard of the same. His intentions and motivations are always good. Simply put, God the Father, God the Son, and God the Holy Spirit will never do anything that is unholy or unrighteous. This is good news because when we are confronted with circumstances, we can be comforted in knowing that He either sent them (that's right, God sends troubles) or allowed them for His good and our perfection. In other words, nothing is happening to you right now that is beyond His goodness and righteousness to address them in a way that He knows will bring Him glory and you are good.

God is reliable and trustworthy. In His own words, He says, "*I, the Lord, do not change*" (Malachi 3:6). That God is immutable should be the best encouragement ever when we are faced with circumstances beyond our control.

There are so many other attributes of God that I could not even begin to cover in this book. The ones I highlighted are those I find encouraging. If you want to learn more about the character of the one true God, I encourage to do a study on His attributes. Start with a website that I have come to rely on in my own personal Bible study: www.ligonier.com. As you learn more of Christ, I am sure you will not be disappointed with who He is and wants to be to you.

CHAPTER 3

Walking in God's Favor

From a secular standpoint, the word favor can be defined as gaining approval, acceptance, or special benefits. It can even mean supporting or liking someone or something and showing an act of kindness beyond what is due. Contrarily, favor in the economy of God has nothing to do with whether we are liked or not. Favor is all about what *God does*, not what we do. Sometimes God's favor comes in the form of His giving us the ability to do something which is humanly impossible for us to do. The most important thing about His favor is that it is unmerited. For example, it is only by God's unmerited favor that we can experience eternal life, because of Christ paying the penalty of our sins on the cross, and it is only God's grace that we can live for the Lord.

I do believe that God's favor is intangible; it is where we have the blessing of God over our lives. I am not saying that life will not present struggles at times, but we must believe that good things will happen. There are so many people who do not expect anything good to happen in their life. If we expect God's favor and declare it, thank Him when he blesses us, and see good things happening in our lives, then we will see even greater blessings from God.

Favor is something given to us by God that no one can take away. It outweighs every opposition that may come against you. When you walk in God's favor, the path you take may not be easy at times, but it is the one He has predestined and predetermined for you. The path God has for each of us will always work in our favor, as it unlocks our full potential and helps us find the gifts and talents that the Holy Spirit has given us.

The favor of God will bless you beyond compare. God's favor positions you in a place where you will lack nothing and be exalted. There may be times when favor puts you on a great platform and positions you for greater influence with decision makers. It did for David before he was named king of Israel. God gave him favor with the then king of Israel, Saul. When he was still an unknown shepherd boy, David became Saul's favorite musician. Eventually he became his armor-bearer and greatest warrior and gained the notice of the entire country. *"A man's gift maketh room for him, and bringeth him before great men" (Proverbs 18:16).*

Favor can proceed from generation to generation and last beyond your lifetime into the lives of your children and grandchildren. God's favor cannot be duplicated, taken away, or used against you. Thank God each day for His amazing grace, love, mercy, and favor over your life. I cannot thank God enough for the favor He has extended to me and my family and the good that comes to us daily.

God's favor outweighs any opposition, any attack of the enemy and any doubt. *"Surely, Lord you bless the righteous; you surround them with your favor as with a shield" (Psalms 5:12 NIV).* The favor of God brings unimaginable new opportunities. Therefore you can walk in victory with pride and faith, for God sees you and knows all about your needs and has promised to fulfill them. For this reason alone, I encourage you to remove all self-doubt, self-pity, and fear from your mind and replace them with self-confidence, belief, and trust in the Lord.

As for me, I am incredibly grateful to God for the favor He has shown me over my life. In fact, He extends his favor to us all each day by showing new mercies and giving us a fresh start.

CHAPTER 4

Remember, you are Graced for It.

It does not matter that you have made a few mistakes or many mistakes, even if you are having regrets, you still have God's grace. In common Christian teachings, grace is unmerited mercy and favor that God gave to humanity by sending His son, Jesus Christ, to die on a cross which secured man's eternal salvation from sin. This kind of grace, as well as love, is eternal and will never be taken away. This was evident in the book *Acts 14: 19-22*, after Paul was stoned–which, some believe, was to death–he received prayer and he was completely healed. We know this because it says that the following day, he went on to Derbe, which was sixty miles away. No man who endured what he went through, would not have been able to walk 60 miles. This is a great example of how God gives you everything that you need to be victorious in any situation, because you are covered by the blood of Jesus and given grace.

Salvation comes by grace alone, by faith alone in Christ alone. Because we are saved by grace, we are no longer under any law that calls for punishing or judging us. Now, that is the beauty of grace, dear friend, as *given* to us by God. We do nothing to get it. Otherwise, it would not be grace. We have been given grace by God to handle anything that comes our way. Aside from that, we have been graced in many areas of our lives to serve God, to operate in our gifts, to overcome situations, to prosper and to forgive. It is by God's grace that we are here to tell our own story and continue to live and walk by faith and not by sight. God has placed in us the ability to withstand unimaginable things with the strength we never thought we had and the confidence to overcome the impossible.

God's grace is sufficient, and his mercy is everlasting. Therefore, we have what it takes to be "more than conquerors" through Christ. *"My grace is sufficient for you, for my power is made perfect in weakness. Therefore, I will boast even more gladly about my weaknesses, so that Christ's power may rest in me" (2 Corinthians 12:9, NIV).* We find in this Scripture that God is telling Paul that He has already given him everything he needs to be victorious in any situation. Likewise, God's grace is His power given to us in the middle of our weakness, because when we are weak, God is strong in us. The word of God assures us in Psalms 46: 1-3 where it says that God is our refuge and strength, and our present help in trouble (NIV). This means that we can always look to God for strength in our time of need. With God as our strength, it is up to us to trust Him and believe in His love and power.

By the grace of God, you can withstand more than you give yourself credit for. *"Let us then approach with confidence, so that we may receive mercy and find grace to help us in our time of need" (Hebrews 4:16, NIV).* Yes, you will experience tough moments throughout your life, but deep inside of you there lies strength that was given to you by God. Again, this is due to the grace of God which gives us the ability to be overcomers.

CHAPTER 5

God's Plan for You

Some of us can be our own worst critic wherein we sometimes place more weight on ourselves than we know, which can make life that much more difficult. When that happens, remember to encourage yourself. God has already set the pace for the outcome of the circumstance, so just continue to trust in Him and believe and receive what He has for you. His plan will never fail you. God has already predestined and predetermined your future, and He knows all about your struggles and shortcomings.

God's plan will never fail, end, and fall short because of His awesome power and glory to fulfill all things in *His* time. He rules over all things. God has placed before us all instructions to follow which are found in His holy word, the *Holy Bible*. Invariably, the Bible has instructions for any situation that may come our way. God's plan includes words of wisdom, guidance, and most of all how to enact faith. The plan to be the best that we can be and to be a blessing to others. God's plan for you is to live in good health and make the right choices in life, choices that will be imperative to your life and to the lives of your family and loved ones. *"For God has not given us the spirit of fear, but of power and love and of a sound mind" (2 Timothy 1: 7 NKJV).*

I know that at times we may question God's plan and ask why His plan differs from the plans we think are right for us. Admittedly, there is a huge difference between our plan and that of God. Our plan can and will fail, but God's plan never fails. God's plan outweighs any attack of the enemy and it will prevail over any situation or circumstance. *"For I know the plans I have for you, declares the Lord, plans to prosper you, and not harm you, plans to give you hope and a future" (Jeremiah 29: 11 NIV).* The ultimate plan of God does not need to be mapped out, designed, or restructured. This is a plan that cannot and will not fail; it cannot not be altered or destroyed.

God's plan for your life has been predestined and, therefore, *no one* can alter it. Everything you have been through and everything you are going through is God's plan for you to prosper (i.e., according to His definition and standard of prosperity), to teach you, and to make you spiritually stronger and equip you with strength in ways you had not been. Things may have not gone well in your life, but God has forgiven you, saved you, and will use your story for His glory. For example, you may be going through something or have been through tough times in your life, where you had nowhere to turn and no way out. Then suddenly, a miracle happened, and everything fell into place. That was all done by God, making all things work for His glory and your good (Romans 8:28). This glory of God's as seen by the outcome of your circumstance will help others and encourage them not to give up and not to give in, but most of all, it will help strengthen a person's trust in God.

God's plan is for you to live a successful life and glorify him for his mighty power. God will not allow anything to happen to you before your time, because His work in you is not complete. You were created by God for His purposes, one of which is to give Him the glory in all you do. I know that this is true, and I am a living testimony to this because when I was broken by alcohol addiction and battling to keep my sanity, I turned to God. With all the sincerity I could muster, I prayed and cried out to Him. In return, He showed me that He was in control. I believe He allowed me to go through those things to teach me and show me that I did not have the power to overcome my situation alone. God showed me that His power outweighed any opposition. *"Therefore, I tell you, whatever you ask for in prayer, believe that you have received it, and it will be yours" (Mark 11: 24).*

CHAPTER 6

Continue to Move Forward

There may be times when you feel like nothing is going right and the whole world appears to be against you. If that happens, keep moving forward even when you are not sure where you are heading.

We often look so long and so regretfully upon a closed door that we do not see the one that is opening for us instead. God will open doors for you, but if you do not walk through them, you have no one to blame but yourself. As for those times when God closes a door, do not try to open it. Believe it or not, this is the same as moving forward because you are not stagnating in a pity party over the circumstance. Instead, you are looking at things as an opportunity to keep going. Then, too, if you try to open a closed door, you may just be revisiting that dark and stagnant place which God brought you out of.

Continue to move forward and seize every moment, every blessing, and every chance you get. You are stronger than you give yourself credit for. Reach for inner strength given to you by God, who gives strength to all. *"Behold, I will do a new thing; now it shall spring forth; shall ye not know it? I will even make a way in the wilderness, and rivers in the desert" (Isaiah 43: 19 KJV)*

God wants us to experience continuous restarts, rebirths, and rebranding in our lives, because He never meant for this life that He has given us to be boring, but for us to live and experience an exciting and purposeful life, to be a blessing to others and rejoice in his glory.

Continue to move forward, and if you need to look back, it is okay. Just do not stay there. Take the pain of your past and learn from it. Starting today, continue to move forward and allow God to lead and guide you to your destiny. *"That men may know that thou, whose name alone is Jehovah, art the most high over all the earth" (Psalms 83:18).*

CHAPTER 7

Do not Let the Devil Steal Your Joy

The devil cannot steal your joy—that is, if you recognize that you alone, and not Satan, are in control of our own joy and your own attitude. As Abraham Lincoln once said, "People are about as happy as they make up their minds to be." In other words, your attitude towards life, even if it has misfortune, things that come against you and other irritants of each day are yours alone. Simply put, not even the devil, your boss, or anybody else, or anything, for that matter, can take your joy unless you allow them to.

One of Satan's most effective weapons for stealing our joy is during those times when we allow ourselves to brood, stew, fret, and fuss over a disservice that someone did to us. Forgiving others is the single most important thing we can do to be happy. This can be accomplished through the mighty power of prayer. And by reading God's word, we allow the Holy Spirit to renew our minds daily, clearing it of negativity and bad thoughts.

The joy that God gives is like no other; it makes us feel good within and gives us a sense of pleasure. *"And the angel said unto them, fear not: for, behold, I bring you good tidings of great joy, which shall be to all people" (Luke 2:10, NIV).*

Joy is an emotion that comes from within. Some people have endless joy, and they spread that joy to others simply by their presence. Joyful people tend to light up a room and make others feel better when they are depressed or having a bad moment. That is the kind of faith we should have, that allows us to see past all our circumstances and trust in God. There is never a time when we can say we have enough faith.

CHAPTER 8

Focus on Your Destiny

Avoid dwelling in the past, dream for the future, and concentrate on the present. When you continue to dwell in the past, there is no chance for a future. Let go of the people and the things that try to stop you or block you. Do not dwell on those who let you down; cherish those who hold you up.

Take comfort in this: your destiny has already been determined by God. He wants you to walk towards it and stay focused, no matter what. We serve a big God, who will give us the desires of our heart as they align with His will for our lives and with His word. So, what is it that you desire? How does it align with God's word? Remember, the disciple James, the Lord's brother, tells us that when our desires are amiss (i.e., having nothing to do with God's will or His word), then our prayers are pointless and will not be answered in the affirmative. Meanwhile, do not lose focus of your goals, dreams, and aspirations that have been graced by the Spirit of God.

Focusing on one thing at a time gives you clarity to accomplish goals that you never would have imagined you could complete. While I believe God has a blessing tailored just for you, I still believe it is important that you continue to stay focused, run the race, contend for the faith, and be of good courage. This is how your destiny is reached in honor and integrity that pleases God and speaks to your character. Continue to seek God and His kingdom, be obedient, and focus on His word. *"But seek first his kingdom and his righteousness, and all these things will be given to you as well"* *(Matthew 6:33 NIV).*

Focusing on your destiny allows you to clear your mind and be renewed in your spirit, which strengthens your faith in Jesus Christ who is the author and finisher of our faith. *"Fixing our eyes on Jesus, the pioneer and perfecter of faith. For the joy set before him he endured the cross and sat down at the right hand of the throne of God"* *(Hebrews 12:2 NIV).*

Continue to trust in God and focus on your journey and destination. God will open the doors that you cannot. Do not get weary or tired. Do not stop or procrastinate. Rather, remember that every step forward brings you closer to your destiny and defeats doubt, so stay focused. Continue to pray for strength during your journey, and, most of all, trust in our Lord and Savior Jesus Christ.

CHAPTER 9

Yes, You Can!

Take a moment to recall those things you wanted to do in your life, heights that you wanted to reach, places you wanted to go. Some of you may be reminded of how quickly your mind told you, "No way! That is not for me. I just cannot do it." Ever wonder why we are so quick to say "I cannot" without even having to struggle to think otherwise? But to say "I can" is it like pulling your teeth? It should not be so, because we can do all things through Christ who gives us strength to do the things that He has called us to do. In fact, His own Spirit is that power within us and enables us to accomplish what Christ put us on earth to accomplish.

Getting to the point where you feel you *can* do something is not easy to come by. It takes faith, which you may lack. You should know that for faith to grow, it must be worked out day and night. This is the only way you can expect to live in peace—with a faith at work and a mind always fixed (i.e., focused) on Jesus.

Here is another piece of advice to attain that *yes, I can* attitude. Maintain a humble spirit and an attentive spirit to hear the word of God and submit to it. We need to keep our minds fixed on him, love people and share the love of Christ with this dying world. When we exercise the two qualities of faith and humility daily, we have the strength to say, "Yes, I can!" It may seem hard, but with God, be assured that you can do all things.

In my case, I am confident that He strengthens me, anoints me, ordains me, leads me, and keeps me. I can and I will do what He has called me to do. This is the attitude that you, too, must have because you can, and you will overcome. You can and will do what God called you to do. You can and you will prosper (i.e., according to how Jesus defines prosperity and success). You can become a blessing to others and be content in this life. Remember this: you only live once, and you can either live a blessed life in the will of God or you can live a mediocre life according to your own will. The choice is yours. Yes, you can choose to do right, and you can choose to live right. You are not alone. God is there to strengthen you and keep you as He says in His word. *"I can do all things through Christ who strengthens me" (Philippians 4:13).*

CHAPTER 10

Keep Hope Alive

It is easy to lose hope when your troubles overwhelm you. Uncertainty and doubt can fill you with fear, especially when there seems to be no way out of your pain and suffering. Jesus told us in his word that we would *most definitely* have many troubles here on earth. He knew what was to come. However, Jesus also wanted us to know that despite our problems, we can stand firm knowing that He has overcome the world. He is the hope of all things impossible. He is the restorer of dreams and has the power to overcome obstacles. There is nothing that can crush a true believer because all the force of heaven lives in the heart of those who belong to Christ. If necessary, a royal army stands ready to fight for you. Jesus is our strength to overcome all that comes against us. It is sad to watch people turn to substance abuse, for example, to silence their pain, something I once did for a quick route to peace.

Unfortunately, many people sell out their hope to alcohol or drugs. They become bonded to the very poison that is destroying their lives and that of their families. It can happen to anyone, by the way. Many people are secretly suffering with addiction, stress, and storms in their lives. They feel lost and out of control because they are trying to carry the burden on their own. That will never bring victory because Jesus never meant for you to fight your battles alone. *"No temptation has overtaken you except what is common to mankind. And God is faithful; he will not let you be tempted beyond what you can bear. But when you are tempted, he will also provide a way out so that you can endure it"* *(1Corinthians 10:13 NIV).*

CHAPTER 11

Nothing Can Stop You or Block You

There is nothing that can stop God's blessings for you in your life. The blessing is an invisible force designed by God to bring us victory and favor in every area of our lives. God's blessings always accompany His presence in any situation, circumstance, or storm. God will neither leave you nor forsake you. Wherever God's presence was in the *Old Testament*, there were great blessings there. Consider the biblical, historical account of a man named Obed-Edom and what happened to him when the presence of the Lord was among him and his family. *"Now Kind David was told, "The Lord from has blessed the household of Obed-Edom and everything he has, because of the ark of God." So, David went to bring up the ark of God from the house of Obed-Edom to the city of David with rejoicing" (2 Samuel 6:12 NIV).* Similarly, in your case, nothing can stop or confine the unlimited, irreversible blessings of God on your life. As we grab hold of this revelation, your faith will soar. Expect the favor of God, the will of God, and the empowerment to succeed in every God-ordained area of your life. With the love God has for you, nothing can stop you.

Whatever you do in Christ Jesus, do it unapologetically. Do not get discouraged by criticism or chatter because people will be people and they *will* talk about you. When people envy you, it may be because they are jealous of you or they may talk about you. Use that as fuel and continue to move forward to achieve whatever God has for you, because nothing is impossible where God is concerned.

Live your life today and do not concentrate on things you cannot control. Tomorrow will take care of itself. *"Therefore, do not worry about tomorrow, for tomorrow will worry about itself. Each day has enough trouble of its own" (Matthew 6:34 NIV).*

CHAPTER 12

You Have the Victory

God's word teaches you that every Christian will face many trials and disappointments in their lifetime, and God promises to deliver you from them all. What comes to mind is the word victory. Generally, victory means a triumph over something, a glorious conquering of some nagging circumstance. No matter how bad things may seem in your life, you will always have victory if you continue to hold on, trust in the Lord, fight and pray. With that said, I want to make it clear what *victory means biblically* so that you do not become confused by this word as you apply it to whatever is going on in your life.

To begin, this word has everything to do with how we stand *positionally* with Almighty God. King David could be assured of victory from circumstances, even the guilt of sin, because of his standing as a servant of the Holy God. The same holds certain for every believer in Christ Jesus. Read how Stanley D. Gales puts it in *Battle of Our Lives*.

The point is this: our victory is in Christ. Our strength is in Christ. Our position for spiritual warfare is union with Christ. We are to "be strong in the Lord and in the strength of his might." We are strong in Christ as we abide in Him, living in His victory and living it out by the Spirit of the risen Christ who unites us to Christ and empowers us to serve Him (Col. 1:9–14), walking in light rather than the darkness from which we have been delivered (Eph. 5:1–18).

I dare say that most of what we go through can be traced to spiritual warfare, a victory our Heavenly Father wants us to win, though we cannot fight Satan as our Lord Jesus did and will again someday when he reins in that dragon, deceiver, liar, and fake forever. Any battle between Satan and Christ is to show us how strong Jesus is over anything and anybody because His magnanimous strength is far above that of all others. Where we are concerned, God will not leave us alone to battle this devil and what he brings our way. He assures us of victory in His Son and our Lord, Jesus Christ. Every one of Satan's tactics, accusations, words, and temptations can be thwarted by what Christ did for us on the cross. The shed blood of Jesus brings victory over them all and keeps us positionally in Him as a child of God. Notice I said "in Him" because when we must move outside of Christ's word and His holiness, victory is not assured. God will only stand by His own way and holiness when answering any petition of ours. So, as we face sin or even trials that come from spiritual warfare, we are to respond as Paul instructs in Ephesians. We are to put on the full armor of God, that is, we are to confront sin and anything else by the word of God and only the word of God (see Ephesians 6).

Victory can come in many forms, such as conquering a fear, victory over an illness, in a competition, and over the devil. The instance God is most concerned about is that we have victory over sin and every wrongdoing, for when sin is ignored, it multiplies and morphs into greater corruption. *But thanks be to God, which giveth us the victory through our Lord Jesus Christ" (1 Corinthians 15: 57).*

Some teach falsely that God has placed in you the victory, the power, and the ability to overcome *any* situation and prosper, to always be an encourager, and to do nothing but win, win, win. While this false teaching sounds good and exciting, the truth of the matter is this: it is misleading and presumptuous. We do not always win at everything, every time. However, the good news is that God has given us his Holy Spirit to win at overcoming sin. And the path to this victory comes by sanctification, which is a life-long process, my brothers and sisters.

God may grant you victory in something today, but His lesson for you tomorrow is that you suffer a loss to understand something greater about Himself and His word. I realize this is the not the kind of victory many people may want to hear, but it is true. As the word says, we may have plans, but it is God and God alone who says whether they will take place or not. The victory in this, if you will, is the peace that comes from knowing that the Sovereign God of all knows what is best and will ensure that it happens. Until victory comes in whatever form and degree that God chooses, I encourage you to continue to strive to be that person God created you to be, without fear, without doubt, and without condemnation. *"With God we will gain the victory, and he will trample down our enemies" (Psalms 60:12 NIV).*

CHAPTER 13

The Choice is Yours

As the saying goes, life is about making choices—whether good or bad. I can recall the many bad choices I have made in my life, but I thank God for His amazing grace and mercy that they will not get the best of me. Let me explain.

Our Christian walk in Christ is fraught with heated battles around making right choices instead of the ones that bring destruction. Now, if God were to judge you on the bad choices, more specifically sins, instead of on what His Son did for you on the cross (i.e., taking on your sins and being judged accordingly), you would be in danger of eternal damnation and without hope. But thank God for His love and forgiveness for the sins we all have committed. He has given you the power (the Holy Spirit) to change and make the right choices and to make righteousness a way of life.

With that said, I want to throw caution to wind. While we all love the total, undeniable freedom to make choices that we think befit our lifestyle, homes, children, jobs, employees, employers, health, etc., the Bible clearly warns that our choices *will bear* consequences. Whatever a man sows, he will reap it. He who sows wickedness reaps trouble" (Proverbs 22:8). Righteousness (right living) is what brings blessing: "Keep my commands and you will live" (Proverbs 7:2); and sin brings judgment. The hard truth is that what we choose to do will affect a corresponding result. Such is the will of God who *always* gets His way. Case in point: many couples choose to live together as man and wife before making a commitment to one another via marriage. God's word is clear about this. We dignify sex through marriage only. Anything outside of that may bring the consequence of sexually transmitted disease or divorce in the case of a person who cheats on their spouse. When we consistently make choices without the consideration of God's counsel on a thing, He, in turn, can choose to give us over to the power these bad choices bring (see Romans 1:18-32). In simple terms, when we rebelliously choose to go our own way, God will allow it as well as the punishment that comes with disobedience.

Obviously, you make choices every day and with God's help, you have the power to change your life. Contrary to popular motivational speaker Joel Osteen, there is no such thing as "a better you" without the saving grace of Jesus Christ ruling your life, including the decisions that you make. In His word, Jesus promises never to leave us or to let anything we do or anything others do to us separate us from His love. That is awesome news! Because that means the bad choices, I have made that led me to sin against the throne of God can be forgiven and will not stop Jesus' interceding to the Father on my behalf (see Romans 8).

Finally, in the event the choices you made begin to weigh heavy on you, remember that you will always have Jesus Christ to confide in and His Holy Spirit to lead you, guide you into truth (i.e., *His* truth about a thing), and strengthen you. *"The tongue of the righteous is choice silver, but the heart of the wicked is of little value" (Proverbs 10: 20 NIV).*

CHAPTER 14

Providence is on Your Side

No doubt you have heard Nationwide Insurance's jingle about the company being "on your side." Through this commercial, the fifty-five-year-old insurance giant would have you believe that no matter the circumstance, presumably Nationwide has got your back! Well, in their minds, that may be true, but there is something that Nationwide can *never* do, but God can—easily, effortlessly and like clockwork, every day because He is the Lord God Almighty overall and for all time. I am talking about His sovereignty, an important attribute of His that influences our perspective of whether we are going to have a good day or a bad day. Let me explain.

The governance of God, which, in everyday speech, is called providence, means that He is the one who directs and cares for *everything* in the universe every single millisecond—all at the same time. That means you, me, your momma, your daddy, your mean-spirited boss, Congress, the president, every single dictator in the world, the repairman who ticked you off the other day, the affairs of every country, successes, failures, all contingencies, the weather, the seasons, angels, demons, and Satan himself, come under the watchful eye of the Lordship of God (see Psalm 103). He is in complete control of everything. He is *the* sovereign (i.e., supreme ruler), as King David once called Him (2 Samuel 7:18-22, 28, 29). Therefore, there is absolutely nothing that gets by Him—even the things we struggle with day after day. He knows about them and will use them for His glory. Why? Because He is the one who calls things forth in the first place, including troubles that we are facing right now. Calling things forth comes under the *sole* authority of God alone (Romans 4:17), an attribute of His glory which He will *never* share with created beings.

How is God's sovereignty good news for us? It means that our lives are not governed by chance or fate. Sure, we all have a free will—the right to make choices. And admittedly there is sin in the world, even though God hates sin. So, then, why would He not only allow us free will but also sin in the world, knowing that our free will could oppose His own and sin, obviously, would counter His holiness? I believe it is because He knows that as the sovereign of everything, there is nothing a created being can do to stop Him from triumphing as the God of the universe. Even the Lord Jesus told the Apostle Paul that continuing to persecute the church and resist Him was a waste of his time because the Lord God would eventually have His way in Paul's life. And how did God get Ruth, a grandmother of Jesus Christ, to Bethlehem, Judea? Well, He called forth the death of her husband, father-in-law, and brother-in-law, along with a famine to hit her hometown. These events would eventually drive her and her mother-in-law Naomi to Bethlehem where Ruth would eventually meet and marry Boaz, a blissful union which had already been divinely mapped out by God.

Here is one last example I want to share about God's sovereignty, though it is a touchy, sensitive one. My ancestors, and those of many of you reading this book, were called to this country, albeit under the evil of slavery. Whatever God's providential reason for our involuntary migration, He orchestrated our becoming citizens of this country—and even to lead the United States as executors in the White House—attain the American Dream and become one of the most educated and successful group of people on the face of the earth. What started in enslavement ended in triumph for a people group that, 400 years ago, was not meant to be successful in anything.

I mentioned all the examples above because I want you to rest easy with this: you can never do anything to thwart the sovereignty of God. Mind you this is not a license to sin against him; rather it is meant for encouragement in case you think you will never be able to crawl out of that pit you may be in right now. Take courage; there is no pit too deep for His long reach. He knows where you are—figuratively and literally. His divine purpose will be met concerning you because He is God, the sovereign of all. He is for you, not against you (see Romans 8).

CHAPTER 15

Attitude is Everything.

Throughout my life, I can honestly say that God has delivered me from many things, but the one thing I am profoundly grateful for is that God delivered me from my evil ways and a bad attitude. My attitude was so bad that I would be evil towards people for no reason at all. I had the worst attitude ever, and by my indulging this nasty attitude, I missed out on great opportunities. For instance, I missed out on being a part of great relationships, job opportunities, and many more blessings. As I grew older, I came to realize that by having a bad attitude, I was not going to experience great successes and this attitude would threaten my ability to reciprocate love because you cannot love anything with an evil heart.

Today I know that my attitude influences the level of my altitude. Just as an airplane cannot fly high and well if it needs repairs, neither could I soar with a negative attitude. Like that plane, I will be grounded until the proper repairs are made. Specifically, my heart and mind needed repairing. I finally realized that I was broken spiritually. I could not heal myself and certainly no physical doctor could heal me. I never lost my belief in the Lord. I am the one who strayed away from Him because God never leaves us. Once I started to pray and trust in the Lord, He began to work inside of me. Through reading and receiving God's mighty word, I began to transform and be the man he called me to be. My attitude improved. I began treating people with the love and respect they deserved. I replaced hate with love, bitterness with kindness, and evil with compassion.

I thank God for never leaving me, even when I left Him. I am thankful for deliverance and healing, love, and forgiveness of my sins.

In essence, I have learned that no matter how I feel about myself, I cannot treat people badly. My life is a result of how I live it and what I think of myself. I think this is a good place for you to stop and read Ephesians, Chapters 1-3. These chapters tell us who we are in Christ. I could write more words to tell you not to think poorly of yourself; however, the real difference comes when you accept *what Christ says* over anyone else's words. Whatever Jesus Christ says is the attitude we must have in life so that we can be all that God called us to be. *"No one will be able to stand against all the days of your life. As I was with Moses, so I will be with you; I will never leave you nor forsake you" (Joshua 1:5).*

CONCLUSION

In my final words, I pray that you do not become intimidated, fearful, or terrified when going through difficult situations in life. Whatever happens, you are graced for it, and you are stronger than your fears and braver than any circumstance— all because of the power of the Holy Spirit in you. And, with His help, you can outlast any attack of the enemy, so continue to believe for victory over defeat. Nothing can stop the promise of God to be with you no matter what. *"Do not be afraid, because I'm with you; don't be anxious, because I am your God" (Isaiah 41:10).*

As I have been saying all along, God has given you the power to prevail, to overcome and remain steadfast, unmovable in any situation or storm. Continue to ask the Holy Spirit to renew your mind daily, then trust in the word of God and his plan for your life which means that all will work out well for your good and His glory (see Romans 8:28). Your future has already been predetermined and predestined by God, and therefore, *no* demonic force can stop you or block you. No matter where you are in life, even in your darkest place, never give up because God loves you and He will never leave you.

Continue to live the amazing life that God has given you and live it to the fullest. I encourage you to continue to let the light of Christ shine through you as you continually put your trust in God. Pray for deliverance from the enemy of your soul, as well as for strength and guidance from the Holy Spirit. Because you are a child of the Almighty God, rest assured that He will give it to you.

I thank God for giving me the ability and the opportunity to write this book and share my story that may be an encouragement to someone. I pray that my words of encouragement and especially the uplifting word of God make a difference in how you approach the low moments that *will* come. I also hope that my story is compelling enough to motivate someone to seek God and for healing from addictions.

Finally, I want to thank the Lord Jesus for reaching down and grabbing me and saving me from myself when I was drowning in sin. You were right there all along to lead me out of darkness and show me the way. I am forever grateful. With all my love to the One and Only Jesus, your servant, Ebenezer.

ABOUT THE AUTHOR

Ebenezer Tyner III, also known to many as E.B. Tyner, is a proud United States Army veteran who served selflessly for over 21 years before retiring in 2003. Ebenezer is a husband, father, grandfather, leader in his church, and a business owner. Ebenezer has been married to his beautiful wife, Latonia Tyner, for 16 years and counting. She is his biggest supporter and encourager. Together they have five children, ranging in ages 20 years to 37 years. He also has nine-year-old and five-year-old granddaughters, with one more grandchild on the way. Family is everything to E.B., and he thanks God for them each day.

Ebenezer loves to encourage people because he believes we all have trying and challenging times, but we do not have to stay there. His passion for encouraging others stems from his own life experiences and how the Lord delivered him from alcohol addiction and depression to be the man God called him to be. Ebenezer has a Facebook page with well over 1,000 members. The page is appropriately named *"Encouraging Words for Encouraged People"* for the purpose of encouraging and uplifting others who may be going through a tough time in their life or providing an encouraging word to make one's day a little bit better through words of encouragement.

Ebenezer holds an associate degree in the field of business administration from American Intercontinental University, a technical certification in electronics technology from IVY Tech State College, and U.S. Army training from Communications U.S. Army Signal School, Ft. Gordon, Georgia. Additionally, he received numerous awards and medals for his service in the U.S. Army.

ACKNOWLEDGEMENTS

I want to thank my beautiful and caring wife, Tonia, for supporting me in the process of writing and publishing my first book. She has had my back for so many years, and I love her dearly. I also want to acknowledge my children who put up with me throughout this arduous process and cheered me on every step of the way. I love you all forever.

Additionally, much appreciation to Mr. Michael Yarborough of Cinema One Films for the awesome photos www.cinemaonefilms.com, to Mr. Jonathan McDougald of J. Alexander Online for the amazing front and back book covers. www.jalexanderonline.com, and a special thanks to my professional and proficient editor Yovonne Perry, for pushing me, teaching me, and being there for me during this process. Each one of you were instrumental in working on and finishing every detail of this book. I am forever grateful to every single one of you.